Rebuilding Your Dream

Family Life with a Disabled Child

by Rhonda Krahl

Support for production of this book was provided by:

The Division of Developmental Disabilities
Department of Pediatrics
The University of Iowa Hospitals and Clinics
Iowa's University Affiliated Program

and The University of Iowa Publications Department
Campus Stores

Table of Contents

PREFACE

We all have images of the future, images of what life will be like, what we will be doing. We cherish these dreams, these visions of the ideal.

Our visions often include children, children visible in our minds even before birth. These youngsters may be running or laughing. They may be singing in the church choir or even receiving their college diplomas. Our children can do anything, be anything, because they are the children of our minds, the children of our dreams.

But, not all dreams come true. For some of us, the dreams shatter as we realize that our children, our beautiful, perfect children, are not to live outside our own minds. Our children will not be perfect; they will have special needs.

When your child's disability is diagnosed, whether at birth or age 16, it hurts. And it keeps on hurting. You will never truly accept what has happened, but you can and must adjust. You can grasp the pieces of your shattered dream and reshape them into a new dream.

This takes time...time to rebuild your dream, time to see beyond the pain and despair and discover the unique joy you can have with your special child. And during that time each day can be a trial, when you wonder, "What next?" Each day you meet new challenges. Each day you fashion another piece for your new dream.

It's not easy. It can't be. But it IS worthwhile, and, eventually, you will find that you have a new, more flexible dream, one that can adapt to the many changes in your life now and in the future.

Drawing by Tyler Leeper, age 4

CHAPTER 1

When it Hurts

Never Prepared

Expecting a child is exciting. No other time is quite like those days of waiting and longing, when you eagerly devote hours to preparing for your new baby. You turn a spare bedroom into a nursery. You buy stacks of diapers, drawers of tiny clothes and shelves of toys and bottles. All this is to assure that you are ready for the new child, and you probably are.

But when your baby arrives, you cannot be prepared for the announcement that he or she has special needs—that something is physically, mentally or emotionally different.

If you have an older child, you make plans for the future. You start saving for college. You buy bedroom furniture that will still be appropriate in 10 years. You keep your old car so your adolescent will have something to drive in a few years. You plan ahead, and then you learn your plans must change.

You cannot be prepared; you must adjust after your child's diagnosis. Whether that diagnosis comes at birth or during childhood, there are many stages in adjusting and many emotions involved. It is a long, difficult process, but you cannot avoid it.

When a child is diagnosed as having special needs, it is something like having twins, only one of whom lived. You expected a normal child, but you did not get one. You dreamed of perfection but the dream did not come true. You grieve for what is not, for what may never be. Of course you're disappointed. That's natural. But while grieving for your lost dream child you can also welcome the child you had not expected. That child is just as precious as the one you prepared for.

Eventually the grief will ease and you will be able to look forward to each new day. But, until that time, you will experience unfamiliar feelings more intense than you thought possible. It's a difficult period, but you WILL survive and you WILL be able to adjust to parenting a child with special needs.

The Days of Disbelief

Denial can be part of adjusting to your new situation. At first, some parents deny that there is anything seriously wrong with their child. Whatever the problem may be, they are sure that it will clear up soon and life will return to normal. Or they accept that their child has a problem, but they are certain that with enough time and effort, they can overcome it. Other parents admit there is a problem, but can't face the potential impact on their lives. All of this is normal. Denying the seriousness of the situation allows you more time to accept the changes in your life. Reality will invade all too soon.

Many Kinds of Fear

Many parents experience fear, especially fear of the unknown. What does all that medical jargon REALLY mean? Are you taking your situation too seriously, or maybe not seriously enough? Will you be able to meet your child's needs, physically, emotionally or financially? What if your child is mentally retarded or does not live?

These are just a few of the fears that can assail you. You don't know what to expect, so you don't know whether to worry or relax, to cry or laugh. You are afraid of the present situation and even more fearful of the future. It's new and it's scary.

Your fears may not be limited to your special child's condition. You may also be afraid for others in your family. You don't know how your mate is going to cope with the situation, and what about your other children? Will they be harmed because you must spend time away from them? Will they feel neglected as you care for your special child? These fears can be especially strong if you are a single parent facing many decisions alone.

Of course, financial worries are often a major concern. Sophisticated medical care is expensive and, in some cases, even routine supplies can be unbelievably costly. Few families are prepared for such bills and immediate solutions may not be available.

Every parent of a special child has fears of some kind. These fears may be simply monsters of the imagination, but sometimes they have a very solid foundation in reality. Yet, without these fears, you cannot be ready for whatever changes are yet to come. Fear is an anticipation of change. Yes, it's new and frightening, but it is a step toward taking each day's events as they come.

Angry at the World

Feeling helpless, parents sometimes lash out at others and even at God. The doctor made a mistake, someone mishandled the child or God is cruel. Anger doesn't solve anything, but it does give parents a way to release some of the pain they feel. Handled properly, anger can be an important part of the adjustment process.

Anger directed at God may be an attempt to find out "why?" Why does your child have a problem? Why does any child have a problem? If God is loving and kind, why are you and your child going through this? It's not fair and you're furious.

You may be angry at a doctor. Why didn't he notice something was wrong sooner? Why did he prescribe that medicine when you were pregnant? He should have been able to cure your child, but he didn't and you're mad. Very mad.

Sometimes friends, relatives or even acquaintances can make you so angry you'd like to hit them. They don't understand how you actually feel, but they certainly know how you should feel. You're overreacting. You're not giving enough attention to your family responsibilities or spending enough time with your special child. Your child would be improving faster if you were doing more. They think you should stop feeling sorry for yourself and devote yourself to your child. These may be the same people who thought you spoiled the child before a problem became evident, but now that things have changed, so have their opinions. It's ridiculous and frustrating.

No one is going to understand exactly how you feel. Even your mate feels differently. Obviously, others you come in contact with have no idea what it's like to cope with parenting a special child, especially if that child's condition has just been diagnosed or changed. They may be trying to help, but all they do is make you angry. Why can't they just keep quiet and leave you alone? If you're angry, that's okay. They would be too in your situation.

Anger Turned Inward

Anger is not always directed at God or others, though. Sometimes anger is directed inward, toward yourself. That's depression. It's normal to feel sad, extremely sad, about your child's condition and its effect on you and those you love. Sometimes, though, that sadness can become too great a factor in your life.

It's natural to cry or lose sleep in trying situations, but if it becomes routine or uncontrollable, you may have a serious problem. Other symptoms of depression are changes in your appetite or sleep patterns. If you suddenly want to eat everything in the kitchen or if you find that the sight of food makes you sick, you may be depressed. If you find you can't sleep or must sleep constantly, that's a sign that something may be wrong. If you have lost interest in life or awareness of what is happening around you, your sadness may have become depression. Of course, some changes are to be expected during times of stress, but if these changes are prolonged or affect your health, you may be depressed.

Depression may be your way of punishing yourself. You are angry with yourself because this child you produced is not perfect. You goofed and you don't like it. Everyone knows now that you made a mistake, a big one. You're not perfect, but you thought you were good enough to produce a normal child. Right?

Although you probably had nothing to do with your child's condition, you may still blame yourself. And, in blaming yourself, you open the door to a lot of questions about your worth. "I can't even have a child right. How can I be good at anything else?" a mother asks. A man feels his masculinity is threatened by having fathered an imperfect child. For those who once saw themselves as strong, resourceful people, the diagnosis of their child's problem takes away the foundation of their confidence. They have always been able to meet challenges, but they are now faced with something new. Something is wrong with their child and they can't fix it. The strong are now weak and they feel inadequate. They have yet to discover the special strengths within themselves, the qualities they never needed before.

Blaming Yourself

Guilt is a common feeling among parents of children with special needs and the other feelings they experience can intensify that guilt. A mother wonders if she did something wrong during pregnancy. Could she somehow have caused the child's disability? A father wonders if his use of alcohol or drugs was to blame. After the diagnosis of an older child, both parents wonder if they neglected to notice something and may accidentally be responsible. Is God punishing them for something? It doesn't matter if the disability was unavoidable. The parents still wonder if they could have prevented it.

They may feel guilty about their feelings toward their child. Resentment can flare because of the changes the child has brought into their lives. There may be financial strain as well as the additional time required to give the child the extra care needed. Parents may wish for the "good old days" before they had to cope with a special child's problems. Anyone in a trying situation wishes for happier times, more acceptable situations. But, for the parent of a child with special needs, such thoughts can lead to guilt.

What To Do

These feelings and others are a necessary part of the adjustment process. They are painful and they may never go away completely. They can return in times of special stress, such as when you receive bad news or your child has been particularly trying. But, there are things you can do to make adjustment easier for yourself, your mate and those closest to you.

One thing that may prove helpful is talking. Just talking. You need someone who will listen without preaching, someone who will not judge you. That person should also care enough about you to let you know when you need more than a friend.

Don't avoid admitting your fears and anger or be afraid to talk about your child's problems. No one can offer you a magical cure, but simply allowing people to show they care can help rebuild your self-confidence and feeling of worth. Voicing your feelings also makes them more concrete. Instead of floating through your mind, they take form. Once they have some shape, they are no longer as frightening and become easier to cope with.

A safe place to acknowledge your feelings is a parent support group. These groups are made up of parents who have children with special needs and who understand the trauma of your situation. They know the despair and anguish you are feeling because they have felt it, too. A parent group is nonjudgmental, a place to express what you are feeling and receive the support and encouragement you need.

If you cannot find someone you trust enough to confide in, try writing down your thoughts. It's not as effective as talking, but it does help you face what is happening.

It's important that you take care of yourself, especially when things are tough. Be sure you get enough sleep, eat regular, nutritious meals and try to exercise each day, even if it's only a walk in a hospital corridor. What your child needs most is a healthy, loving parent. You can give him that by taking care of yourself.

You must also be patient with yourself and others. Having a child with special needs is a new experience for you. Don't expect to feel ready to face the world in a day, a week or even a month. Maybe you will be able to, but you might not. You need time to adjust to your child's disability.

In general, people are caring. They may not understand how you feel, but they know you are hurting and they care about you. They want to help and do so in ways that are comfortable to them. You may not appreciate their advice or even offers of financial help. You may not want their attentions. But accept their overtures in the spirit they are offered. Usually even the most hurtful comment was offered with good intentions. Accept the care and concern, even if you reject the remark. It helps to know people care.

If church has been a part of your life, don't neglect it now. You can find great comfort in faith and the concern of those in your religious community.

If you have hit bottom, don't worry. Sometimes it's nice to forget about all your responsibilities and think about yourself for a while. Give yourself a few minutes to cry, or rave about how unfair life is, how nobody understands or how rotten you are. Then get up, take a deep breath and get on with your life.

You Can Make It

Given time, you can work through these traumatic stages successfully and look forward to a rewarding, fulfilled life for yourself and your family. If, however, you seem to be unable to move on, you may need more than a friendly ear. A social worker or psychologist may be able to help you sort through your feelings.

Remember, a parent of a child with special needs is first of all a person. You have a right to strong feelings about your child's disability. It is only through facing these feelings and allowing them to show you new strengths that you will find the courage to meet each new day.

Drawing by Kristen Hansen, age 6

CHAPTER 2

Marriage With Special Needs

This chapter focuses on maintaining and strengthening a marriage relationship. A strong marriage is a special triumph and source of support in families with a child with disabilities. But it is important to recognize that, like all children today, many children with disabilities will at some time be part of single-parent families. These families face the same challenges that two-parent families face with their own unique set of strengths and needs.

A Fragile Situation

With our current divorce rate as a measure, it's obvious that marriage is a challenge today under any circumstances. It's been said that having a child with special needs won't break a marriage unless cracks are already present. That may be true, but no relationship is perfect. All have cracks and must be protected from the added stress that can come with parenting a special child.

You and your spouse are individuals, with needs and desires of your own. You may have blended them in a fulfilling relationship in the past, but the presence of a child, any child, will change that relationship. No matter how much you both love your child, he or she will create change. If the child has special needs, the changes will be greater and more demanding.

Simply giving the child needed care can take so much time that you wonder how you will get everything done. You never had a problem before, but suddenly you can't seem to stay on track.

Your child's care demands the time that you are accustomed to using for other purposes; time you used to relax or pursue a hobby such as gardening, woodworking or sewing; time you need to wash the car, clean the house or mow the lawn.

With time already at a premium, your child also creates more work for you. Laundry often increases dramatically with a disabled child, especially a baby. Cooking may be a challenge because of unusual dietary needs. And don't forget about preparing the car for all those trips to the medical center. It takes time—time you just don't have.

When our Tom came home from the hospital, he required a LOT of care. His older brother, Tim, was almost two and full of mischief. With the two boys, there were so many demands on my time that I couldn't remember what I had done that day and what I had done the day before. I finally made a chart of 21 daily tasks. It was the only way I could keep track of what I had or hadn't finished.

With all the time you must spend with and for your child, it's easy to forget to take time for your mate. You may see each other at meals or bedtime, but there simply isn't time to sit and talk or do things together. Even your evenings may be filled with necessary, but separate, tasks. You can easily lose track of what your mate is thinking, feeling or doing as you concentrate on keeping up with family routines.

Because you spend less time together, you are less likely to be aware of each other's feelings. Everyone adjusts to having a special child in his or her own way. You may be upset because your wife won't accept the seriousness of a diagnosis that you are furious about. She is in denial; you are angry. There's nothing unusual about this, but if you aren't aware of each other's feelings, you can't be understanding and tolerant.

New Problems

Disagreements may arise over your child's care. Decisions must be made, and you and your mate will not always agree. What then? There will be tension, with neither of you wanting to give in. Often there are alternate forms of treatment, making it difficult to decide what to do. Even if there is no choice, going ahead with something you are uneasy about can make you resentful. Why didn't your mate come up with something else?

Financial difficulties are often a major source of stress. With the presence of a special child can come huge medical expenses, which few families are prepared for. In an already tense situation there are now more worries. Will one or both parents have to change jobs to provide adequate insurance coverage or income? What will you do about child care while you're at work? If your child becomes ill, will you be able to take time off? You suddenly feel guilty about every little luxury, even buying an extra sandwich at the hospital cafeteria. You just don't know where the money will come from to pay the latest bill.

On top of everything else, the physical and emotional demands of parenting a child with special needs can leave you drained, just plain worn out. You can't stop, yet you feel you can't go on. You become so driven by the necessities that you overlook all else—even your mate.

What To Do

There is no easy cure for such stress. But, you are not powerless. You must protect your relationship. First, you must MAKE time for each other. This isn't neglecting your responsibilities. If the relationship crumbles you will face even more duties. Taking time to preserve your relationship makes good, practical sense, even if something else has to suffer temporarily.

Finding this time can be very difficult, so be creative. One couple puts their children to bed just a little earlier while another couple plans naptime for when they are together. During the summer, Gary and I work together canning fresh vegetables from our garden, giving us an opportunity to talk without neglecting our work.

You should also make time to get away completely on occasion. Hire a babysitter and go out to dinner or a movie. If you don't want to spend money on entertainment, go on a picnic or visit friends. Just go somewhere.

If you can leave your child for longer periods, take a short trip. Some parents just go to a nearby motel for a night. They're still close in an emergency, but arc able to take a short break. Whatever you do, try to leave your worries at home. They will be there when you return, but, for a while, concentrate on your mate and you. Rediscover what made you fall in love to begin with.

If you can't afford a babysitter, check with the social worker or nurse at your child's treatment center. There may be a respite care program in your area. These programs sometimes use a sliding fee scale so that all families can afford child care. Also, check with nursing schools. Perhaps there is a student who would be willing to watch your child for a low fee for the experience.

Even when you are at home, TALK to your mate and listen when he or she talks. Really listen. Make the effort to understand what is being said, instead of tuning it out. If you are feeling worried or angry, say so. Say, "I'm mad because..." Don't blame the other for whatever's wrong, but describe how you feel. You don't have to agree, but you do need to understand.

Try to be more sensitive to your mate's feelings. If he or she is upset but won't discuss the reason, be patient. It may have nothing to do with you. Don't pry, but make it clear that you care and are willing to listen.

Learn to be more open about your own feelings. Share your dreams and sorrows. You wish you could spend three glorious weeks in Hawaii with no children and no responsibilities. You wish you had a new sports car. Or you fear that your child's eyes aren't following movement as well as they should. TELL YOUR MATE! These things are an important part of what you feel and how you respond to the world. Share with each other. It will create a common bond that helps hold the relationship together.

Don't neglect the physical side of your relationship. Even a quick hug shows your love. And if your mate is feeling overwhelmed with work and worry, he will appreciate that you care. There is also great emotional relief in intimacy. You may feel that you have to suppress your emotions to keep from losing control, but during sex you don't have that restriction. You can both find comfort in being together.

Parenting a disabled child can be a strain on even the most competent person. Take advantage of having a partner to help. Gary and I try to practice "tag team" parenting. When one of us is ready to crack, the other steps in. Whether it's discipline, physical care or just petty details, we try to give each other a break. Sometimes we are aware that the other is feeling overly pressured or tense and automatically come to the rescue. But sometimes, we must ask for the relief we need. It isn't always easy to admit that we need help, but we have developed a relationship that allows for mutual support.

If financial worries are coming between you and your mate, talk to the social worker at your child's treatment center. He can refer you to agencies and government programs that assist with medical expenses. You can also consult a financial counselor. These people know how to make the most of your assets and still allow you to eat out or go to a movie occasionally without feeling guilty. They can help you make a reasonable, workable budget and still plan for the future.

Getting Help

Not all marriages can survive the stress of a special child. Some would have ended anyway, but others simply break when the tension becomes too great. If you feel your marriage is in serious danger, get help. Talk to your minister or seek counseling from a therapist. Some mental health centers offer sliding fee schedules and time payment plans. You may feel that you can't afford the time or money to take advantage of this counseling, but can you afford not to?

There is no shame in seeking help. Talking to a counselor is simply asking for an objective opinion. He or she is not emotionally involved, and can take an unbiased view of the factors that are pulling your relationship apart. Counselors don't have all the answers, but they can help you understand and make decisions with more confidence.

Reaching Out

Married couples who isolate themselves from all but each other can find themselves feeling desperately alone. It is important to make sure that a spouse does not become the only source of emotional support, the only close relationship. The intensity of need in marriage partners who have isolated themselves can be too great to bear. Close relationships with relatives, friends, members of community groups, such as church or even support groups for parents of children with disabilities are important to the survival of your marriage relationship. For single parents, effective use of these resources will help them feel less alone.

Marriage, like any successful partnership, is the result of two people working together. If yours is to survive, both partners must be willing to become more open and flexible. Though this is important in any marriage, it is vital when a special child is involved. It's worth the effort. You'll be able to share the work and the worry and, best of all, the joys!

Drawing by Heather Wilde, age 10

CHAPTER 3

Frustrations Plus

Normal Frustrations—With a Difference

Parenting any child can be difficult at times. Children have minds of their own—minds that rarely think as ours do. As parents, we must endure these trying situations and hope they pass quickly. Face it—parenting is a tough job. And it's even tougher for parents of children with special needs. We must cope with all the trials inherent in parenting PLUS an extra measure simply because of those additional needs. And because our children have unusual restrictions, they require extra care and supervision. As a consequence, our tempers may be a little short, adding to the problem.

I have two children, only one of whom has a disability; but, I have felt the same frustrations with both of them. As a college instructor told my child psychology class, handicapped children are more LIKE normal children than different. I have found, though, that with a special child, you experience these frustrations more often and they add to the stress you already face because of your child's condition.

A girl with mental retardation has learned to scream or swear when she wants attention. A child with limited use of his legs slides down the edges of the steps, rather than safely lowering from one step to another. One little boy with cerebral palsy loves to sneak out of the house. He knows that by the time his mother catches up with him, they will be half way around the block and will finish the walk—which is what he wanted to begin with. These children aren't exceptionally naughty and their parents aren't neglectful. But their relationship is intensified by the presence of a disability.

If there are times when you feel ready to give up, when you would like to trade your child in for a new model or deny any relationship, you're not alone.

We all know children who whine or cry constantly. They lost a toy, they want a piece of candy, somebody pinched them, they're hungry, they're tired, they want attention. They may not even know what they want, but YOU want quiet, preferably in a separate room. If the child is "normal", his mother or father can seek sympathy from a friend or co-worker. But if that child has special needs, the parents may be ashamed to admit that they need a break or don't know what to do.

One of the most embarrassing situations in parenting is when a child becomes obstinate in a store. When one of my sons cries for something he wants or simply refuses to do whatever is asked, I try to ignore the behavior, telling him that I will continue shopping without him. If the child is Tim, my "normal" son, onlookers may nod with approval at the firm, decisive reaction. However, if that child is Tom, who has an obvious disability, those onlookers are likely to scowl with disapproval at such cruelty.

There seems to be an unwritten rule of parenting a child with special needs: If we can't be patient, loving and understanding at all times, we are BAD PARENTS. Phooey! We have the same frustrations as other parents; we're just not allowed to show them.

Frustration assumes many forms and is as variable as our children. Rare is the child who does not suffer from "mother's ear," that undiagnosable condition in which a child hears everything except what a parent says. Even then, she may be able to hear words like "ice cream," "play" or "puppy." In milder cases, the child hears everything, but can't seem to understand phrases like: "Put on your brace." "Pick up your room." "Take your medicine." These might as well be in a foreign language. But "Let's go to Grandma's" or "pudding for dessert" come through loud and clear.

Children, especially children with special needs, move at a slower pace than parents. One mother claims that if she tells her child, "Get your shoes on. We're leaving in 15 minutes," she'll be lucky to walk through the door in half an hour. Schedules seem to have been invented to provide our children with opportunities to aggravate us. Of course we know the medicine must be given as directed, the diaper should be changed frequently or exercises have to be done regularly. These things are important and must be performed on time. Unfortunately, children's sense of time differs from ours, and, the activity of the moment is more important to them than what you want.. They don't ALWAYS mean to be difficult, they just can't see the urgency in anything other than what they are doing. It's perfectly logical—to a child.

There are times when our children, normal or special, seem to have exceptional abilities—but only for a moment. A child may have trouble with a first grade reader, but, just once, can whiz right through your Christmas shopping list. Maybe your child has difficulty moving, but alone with a dog in the room there is a way to reach its tail. Even poor coordination doesn't prevent a child from finding the tapes that fasten a diaper. These feats would astound a teacher or therapist, but parents are aware of the hidden powers of childish determination.

Your child may also have an unusual sense of humor. You think peas are a nutritious vegetable; your child sees them as textured finger paints. You want to get your child in the car quickly, so you can get out of the cold; your little one, all snuggled in an insulated jacket and hat, thinks it's a great time for a hug break.

A child's values also seem strange at times. If it is important to you that your house always be neat, you will be frustrated by your child's room. To a youngster, there is something very satisfying about playing amidst clutter. If he or she can empty a closet and still find a spot to sit, that's happiness. And, of course, ending such happiness by putting things away doesn't seem right. Whether it's baby toys or remote control cars, books or doll clothes, your child has ideas on how things should be arranged—ideas that probably are not the same as yours.

Get The Facts

Some of your child's behavior may be related to his condition. If you suspect your child's disability or medication may be involved in his or her difficult behavior, talk to the doctor. Other professionals, such as social workers or psychologists may also be able to advise you. It helps you determine methods of discipline and takes away some of the feelings of being a "bad parent" if you know there is a physiological cause for inappropriate behavior. It's always better to narrow down what ISN'T causing a problem, even if you can't find out what IS.

For a time, one little girl had difficulty controlling her temper. Always a charmer in public, she became a volcano at home. Her parents never knew when she would erupt or why. As outbursts became an everyday occurrence, they intensified their search for a cause. Perhaps the behavior pattern was related to her disability. If so, one approach could have been more effective than another. Medication might also have been to blame. Some drugs can cause side effects such as sleepiness or irritability. A malfunctioning shunt in her brain could have been the culprit. Because it was possible that there was a medical cause for the little girl's unusual behavior, her father and mother talked to her doctors. In her case, it was simply a "stage" she was going through, fighting for independence and against her physical limitations. Although there was no quick cure, her parents were able to discipline her without guilt.

What To Do

There are steps that all parents can try in order to relieve the tension in their homes. Other actions work only for parents of children with special needs. And some don't work at all.

First, if the frustration is beginning to overwhelm you, take a break. Get away for a few minutes or a few hours. Hire a babysitter and go out to eat. Stroll around the yard—alone. Sometimes I feel an overwhelming urge to soak in a hot tub of water. It's not that I have a compulsion for cleanliness; it's just my method of escape—and sometimes I feel this need two or three times a day!

One mother has found it helpful to plan a "quiet time" for her children each day. It may mean reorganizing her schedule or priorities, but it's worth it. She puts them to bed a little earlier or sets aside a time for independent play. She takes out the Play-Doh, scissors or crackers. The mess can be cleaned up later, but, for a little while, she can have peace and an opportunity to relax.

You are the best judge of when it's time for a break. Examine your attitude. Are you able to see your child as an individual, precious just as he or she is? Can you see the wonderful person beneath the annoying behaviors? Do you enjoy spending time with your child? If you have come to view your child more as a source of frustration than joy, it's time to take a break. Don't feel guilty, just get away long enough and often enough to be able to value your child as you would a friend.

It also helps to look at the situation objectively. Is your child being especially difficult, or are you especially jumpy? Did the child cause a catastrophe or just make a mess? You have to keep things in perspective.

A sense of humor is also vital to your sanity. Can you find something funny about washing your child's masterpiece off the freshly painted wall, refolding all the clothes or mopping up the lake on the bathroom floor? Is there nothing good about the situation? When all else fails, remember that this will make a great story—in about ten years.

Some parents find relief in physical activity or a hobby that requires concentration. There are times when I actually enjoy scrubbing floors. Gary nurtures a large garden each summer. Exercising can provide an outlet for tension. Reading provides an escape, as does wood-working or other hobbies.

Just Add Love

Sometimes, parents must pay for what happens to their children when they are apart. Grandma and Grandpa often invite Tim and Tom to visit them. And of course the boys are always angels when they go to their grandparents' house. But, when they come home, I know I'll suffer. They save up all their mischief and unload it on me. I used to dread picking them up from Grandma's and Grandpa's. Now I know what to expect and try to stay calm, realizing that things will soon be back to normal.

If your child goes to school or day-care, you may be paying for frustrations there. Is a childcare provider pushing too hard? Are there problems with the other children? Is your child worried about something? If you think school may be partly responsible for your child's unusual behavior, talk to the teacher or someone else on the staff. Parents are often encouraged to visit and observe, something young children enjoy, too.

Sometimes children don't know what's bothering them. They are just grouchy and confused—and frightened by feelings they don't understand.

If your child can't or won't explain why he's behaving the way he is, try simply offering a little extra love and attention. Put whipped cream on the pudding at dinner, just because it's fun. Offer praise for something done well, but don't go overboard. Kids can always sense a phony. Listen to your child read an extra story or let him or her sit on your lap during cartoons. It really doesn't matter what you do. What's important is that your child feels your love and caring. Talk may come or you may never figure out what's wrong. But your understanding will give a sene of safety, making the situation easier for both of you. It also gives you another chance to see the unique person you are nurturing.

Changing Behavior

As with any child, if inappropriate behavior is frequent, dangerous or destructive, it must be controlled.

One step in behavior modification is simply ignoring the problem. If your child screams for attention and is not in any danger, ignore it. If there is yelling or anger, don't respond. He or she may learn that such things aren't going to achieve anything and there are more acceptable ways to communicate with you. Be sure to offer praise if that happens. If you choose this method, however, you should be prepared. Before a child decides to change, the negative behavior will probably get worse. Screaming may be longer or yelling louder before it sinks in that you aren't paying attention.

You can also try staying calm and firm. When a child breaks the rules, give a calm warning about what will happpen if it is done again. Then follow through. Maybe he or she will have to come inside, or sit on a chair, or lose the use of the telephone, or your nightly rocking. The important thing is that you follow through and be consistent. If you feel sorry and change your mind the next time you won't be believed.

In our home, we have a 1-2-3 system. If the boys are doing something they know they shouldn't or have been warned to stop, we simply say, "One." If they don't stop, we say, "Two." If they still don't stop, we say,

"Three." Three strikes and they're out. They know they will be disciplined. We rarely get to three now, and if we do, nothing would have stopped them anyway.

Another method of managing behavior is charting, which has been used successfully in schools for years. You may want to try it in your home. With your child, discuss what goals you think you should work toward. Then make a chart where you can note each time a goal is achieved. The reward could be a gold star, a special privilege or money.

Our boys are expected to complete seven of ten self-care and household tasks each day. If they do so, they earn a quarter. If they make it seven days in a row, they get a 25 cent bonus—a possible $2 a week. It's not a fortune, but sometimes it works. Tim even included "don't hit Tom" on his chart. As the boys have grown older, it has helped to let them know we understand the pressures they face. If their father or I make their beds or pick up their rooms for a day or two, they are more likely to do it the other days. On a day when they have a lot of homework or Gary and I have plans that involve them, we don't expect them to get as much done.

We have also allowed the boys to see just how human their parents are. We now have a third chart on our refrigerator. Gary and I have a list of ten things we should do, but often neglect. The boys keep track of whether the washing and dishes have been done or if business papers have been taken out of the car. We don't get a reward, but the boys feel the system is more fair when everyone is charted.

The goal of any form of discipline is to teach children to control their behavior. Try to explain why something is wrong and what the consequences could be.

Good behavior is a team effort, and parents are the captains of that team. But don't feel you've let the team down by losing your temper. That doesn't make you a failure—it makes you human. Parenting isn't taught; it's learned from "the school of hard knocks."

This Too Will Pass

Sometimes, nothing will work. As a mother, I know. Even the calmest, most responsible parent comes to a dead end where everything seems to have failed. Then there are fewer options. You can try to be patient, hoping it's only a phase your child will soon outgrow. You can scream and cry and look desperately for something, anything, that might work. Or, if the problem is serious and you feel you will not be able to control it, you can consult a child psychologist or social worker who specializes in behavior management.

Whatever you decide to do, don't feel that you're a poor parent. You're not. We all have problems with our children.

It just feels like you're the only one.

Drawing by BJ Leeper, age 10

CHAPTER 4

Brotherly Love

Love, Family Style

If you have more than one child, you know that children fight. They tease; they argue; they even occasionally hit. And jealousy among siblings can pop up at any time. A toy, a little extra attention to a younger child or a privilege granted an older child can lead to mayhem.

Children also have differences with their parents. From leaving toys on the floor to staying up just 10 minutes later, there are plenty of opportunities to differ. It's part of growing up, of becoming independent. It's also irritating for parents.

These are normal situations. ALL kids fight. ALL kids differ with their parents. It's unavoidable. But in families with a disabled child, dissension can indicate a problem. If your children have few periods of peace and friendship or you can't seem to do anything to please them, examine the situation closely. There may be a reason for the excessive conflict.

Through a Child's Eyes

To understand what's happening, you must view the situation through your child's eyes. If children feel slighted, they will seek more attention. If they feel pressured, they'll fight back. You may think they're overreacting, but it's THEIR feelings that are important to them. And, of course, they may not be overreacting. They may be right.

Is your special child getting more attention than necessary? Love and physical care demand a lot of time, but you could be devoting too much time to this one child and neglecting to give other children the time and attention they need, causing them to feel left out, ignored.

What about your special child? Does he or she feel slighted because you made time to go to a junior high football game but couldn't listen to a first reading effort?

Don't play favorites. Do you let your special child do something that your other children are scolded for? Or do you forgive sloppiness from your special child, but condemn it from the others? Handicapped children can't always follow the same rules, but your other children may not be able to understand that.

Or do you allow a younger child to stay up to watch a favorite television show, but tell your special child he or she needs more sleep and must go to bed on time? That's tough on any child.

Children like to help their parents. It makes them feel important and useful. But it's easy to ask too much. Do you expect ALL your children to make their beds neatly, even though one can't stand up to straighten the covers or are your able-bodied children required to help with special care? Are you expecting your children to do more because they have a sibling with a disability? They may have more responsibility than they can cope with, especially during their own personal crises.

And finances are simply beyond the comprehension of most children, especially younger ones. They can't see the difference between necessities and luxuries. They don't even know what bills are. If they see their brother getting everything he needs, they may not understand why they can't have something they want. They can't have the toy that everyone else has, but their brother has a new computer that talks. They can't have a racing bike, but he has a new wheelchair. It just doesn't seem fair.

Your children might resent their handicapped sister because she limits them. They may not be able to do the things they want because of her schedule. Friends can't come over during her nap. You can't take them to the parade because she has had a laxative. Or maybe you can't go to the movie because the theater is inaccessible for her.

Handicapped children also resent their able-bodied siblings at times, and not only for special privileges. It's hard to watch brother or sister running, reading or speaking when they only dream of such freedom. They may wonder why THEY have to be different.

Your children may also be embarrassed by their special sibling. Unusual behavior is barely tolerable in private, but it's humiliating in front of friends. Of course, embarrassment is common in any family, as each member strives to mimic the latest craze. Strange phrases, outlandish behavior or "stylish" clothes can embarrass others in the family. Children, especially adolescents, can be uncomfortable and unforgiving. But this is a greater problem for those with a mentally retarded sibling. And if the retardation is not obvious it's even more difficult.

Your children could also be lonely. They have a brother or sister, but they can't play together like other siblings. My boys couldn't play tag or hide and seek together when they were young. They wanted to be friends, but couldn't develop that friendship the way other children would.

What To Do

These may seem like petty frustrations, but they can accumulate and appear in unexpected ways. Rebelliousness, aggressiveness or even meekness may be your child's way of coping. If you think there is a problem, examine your child's life and habits. Try to find clues to thoughts or feelings. Remember, it's THEIR thoughts that matter.

If your child is old enough, try to explain why you or your special child behave as you do. Explain the inconsistencies, your own limitations.

Also, set aside time to spend alone with each child. Play a game, ride bicycles or go on a picnic together. Just find time away from other children. It will help cement your relationship and give you both a much-needed break.

You don't have to talk on these outings unless you want to. But if your child does talk, listen—really listen. Try to understand how he or she feels and why. You don't have to convert, but you can develop mutual respect for your differences. When I take one of my boys shopping, I spend most of my time listening. I learn things in the supermarket that I would never hear at the dinner table.

As in any family, you must be fair when disciplining. Be sure your able-bodied child is to blame before scolding. If your special child is to blame, make the consequences similar...and don't assume only one child is at fault. You may not be able to use exactly the same discipline with both children, but both need to see that you discipline fairly.

If bickering has become excessive or physical attacks have become frequent, you may need to limit the amount of time your children are together. Let them play together for short periods, praising them when peace reigns. As peace becomes more common, increase the time they are together. You may not need to physically separate the children, just find different activities for them. And you can join in their games at times, enjoying their company while providing a buffer.

If your children seem to be unable to find a joint activity that is practical and interesting for both of them, offer to help. Our boys have managed to adapt most games, but there are still some things that just aren't practical. Often, Tim shows amazing tolerance of Tom's limitations and will graciously accommodate him. Other times, Tim is impatient and chooses not to play Tom's style of baseball or cards.

Try to know your moods as well as you do your childrens'. If you are short-tempered, admit it. One mother tries to warn her children when she is unusually jumpy. Then they at least have a chance to avoid being snapped at. And if you do yell at your children for no reason, don't be afraid to apologize. To err is human, right? You can turn a miserable situation into a good example by showing your children that it is okay to admit your mistakes and that you respect them enough to apologize when you have been unfair.

No matter what your child's limitations, the greatest need is for love. Make sure that all your children realize that you love them as they are. You may not like their behavior, but you love them. Caring for EACH child as an individual, unique person is the basis for healthy relationships. There will always be battles, but they don't have to become wars where no one can win.

Drawing by Tom Krahl, age 13

CHAPTER 5

Keeping It Together

A Delicate Balance

A thriving, vital family is like a balance scale. Peace and dissension may not always balance perfectly, yet neither continually outweighs the other.

But how do you come by this balance? Is there a magical formula? "Mix together two children, two parents, a few friends, then add a healthy dose of support from grandparents." That has worked for my family, but every family is unique and has its own formula.

Not all families have two children or two parents. Grandparents may live far away or be overly critical. And even if the same number of people are involved, each is an individual. Each adds to the balance in a unique way.

You may have blended your particular group of individuals into a thriving family in the past, but with the diagnosis of your child's problem or a change in its status, the formula is altered. Priorities are different. So are schedules and pressures. What worked for your family before may not work now. You must change the formula if you are to regain that balance.

Your family is a vital resource in adapting to your child's special needs. And yet, too often, the family becomes a casualty of the situation instead of a refuge. The worries, pain and fear in each member can lead to isolation, a tendency to try to cope alone. Almost unnoticed, the family as a unit deteriorates into a group of people living separate, lonely lives.

But how do you preserve the family? How can you nurture it when you have all you can handle getting through each day? It seems like one more burden on an already overloaded heart.

Family Is Important

Nourishing the family unit is important for several reasons. First, it IS a refuge. The people you live with care about each other. You have more freedom to deal with your feelings because these people have seen you at your worst. You don't have to put on a happy face. Second, the others in your family are in the same situation. They may not share exactly the same feelings, but they too have been affected by your child's condition. They are the most likely to be accepting of your needs. Third, caring for the family as a whole takes effort. You must be aware of other people and relationships. In doing so, you cannot concentrate on your troubles. You must release some of the attention you focused on your child or your pain. Nurturing the family means taking a break from your private struggle.

An Individual Struggle

Adapting to the presence of a child with special needs is a struggle—for you and everyone else in the family. Each person will react differently, often leading to confusion and misunderstanding. In trying to blend these different reactions into a supportive family, people become more aware of themselves and others. They grow as individuals and become more capable of handling each crisis as it arises.

Your child's diagnosis has changed not only your situation. It has changed you and every other member of your family. As a parent, you now feel greater responsibility. You worry about your child and about forcing a smile for all those people who don't know your world has collapsed. Your children feel stress you aren't aware of.

They also worry about their sibling and feel the pinch of financial strain. They may feel left out as you try to cope, leaving you with less time and energy for them. And what about your special child? Infants, of course, are only concerned with their own well-being. But older children, even toddlers, can feel the frustration of being different or the lash of your impatience.

Individuals struggle to cope with their emotions and the pressure in their own way. In doing so, others may become less important. The cooperation and interaction that once provided stability are no longer present.

One father began drinking heavily, another was incapable of making a decision. The mother of a child with cerebral palsy immersed herself in her profession. Or you may choose isolation, as did a mother who avoided contact with others. For some, hours spent in a workshop or reading helps them cope with a situation they cannot change. A lack of interest in sex or anything involving someone else also separates them. For others, a need for alcohol, cigarettes or food becomes overwhelming.

Your children also cope in individual ways. They too may become more involved in outside activities or suddenly isolate themselves from peers. For older children, alcohol, food, cigarettes or even sex can become a crutch. Bad behavior or open rebellion may be a way for them to deal with a situation they can't understand.

It is so easy to become angry. Just when you need to know that SOMETHING is normal, the people closest to you change. Your loving mate stays out later, leaving you suspicious when you need encouragement. Your baby becomes irritable, crying constantly, just when you feel you will break from pressure. And older children, whom you look to for support and help, are only interested in their friends, their interests, their desires. You need them to be as they were, as you want them to remain. But they can't stay the same, and neither can you.

If the family is to survive, you must reevaluate your perception of each person. Their behavior is obvious, but the reasons for it may not be. Overtime can be a father's way of feeling useful. He can't change the child's condition, but he can have an effect on a new contract or project at work. Over-activity may be a way of denying the entire situation. If you don't have time to think, you don't have to face the problems. For some, the pain is so great that they cannot handle any more stress. They avoid seeing others so they will not have to talk about what has happened. Or maybe they try to escape into the fantasy world of a novel. There are reasons for the way we behave as we do, and often we cannot see them.

Behavior also masks our children's pain. Naughtiness may be a way to be reassured that you still care for them. They may fight for attention or resent their siblings. They also may deny that there's anything wrong. To admit it would mean that they were different from their friends with "normal" families. Anger may hide fear. Your special child may fear death or further illness. Siblings are made aware of the fragility of health—even youth is no barrier to death. And, with the narrow-mindedness of the young, they may resent changes in your financial status.

As family members struggle to survive a frightening situation, they can become simply a group of people who share a house. They may still live together, but the support and concern are gone and without them, the foundation of the family crumbles.

Almost accidently, each person becomes guided by his or her wants, needs, desires. Control over something in life becomes very important. A sense of self-preservation can easily overpower the ability to moderate desires for the sake of others.

It's Up To You

But how do you balance the fears, the pain, the needs of everyone? How do you put all these on the scale and yet make it balance? It's a delicate process, requiring effort and commitment from all members. It takes time to experiment until you discover the balance that works for you—YOU, not the therapist or social worker. YOU know and care about the individuals involved. Only you can make that scale balance once again.

As parents, the primary responsibility for maintaining a balance is yours, even though it may be an unwanted burden at times. You are the adults, the leaders, and you have the power to guide the other members of your family to greater unity.

There is no easy way to honor the individuality of family members and yet encourage the cohesiveness so necessary to them. Each person is concerned with his or her own needs, physical and emotional. People don't want to give up the luxury of self-pity or self-centeredness, because if they do, they may not be able to handle what comes next.

The needs of your special child may seem obvious--extra supervision, medication, regular therapy, help with schoolwork or dressing. These needs are obvious. But there are other needs, too. Perhaps he or she is a child who requires extra love, or solitude, or maybe a physical outlet for frustration and energy. There are many needs that a doctor or therapist can't diagnose. You, as a parent, must develop the insight to realize the hidden qualities and frustrations your child' may not admit.

The needs of your other children are not very different from your special child's. They may not need the extra supervision or physical care, but they still need reassurance of your love and their importance to you. If their sibling is an infant, they may have already had to give up a bedroom or some privacy. Certainly, they've had to give up a share of your time—time they used to tell you their disappointments and dreams. And they may have had to give up some activities because the money or time to support them simply is no longer available. Even if you have great kids who have taken such sacrifices in stride, they could still be hurt or disappointed. And don't forget, they care for their brother or sister, too. They share many of the pains he or she feels.

But even the most creative parents cannot always find such easy solutions. They have to ask for a little extra cooperation from others. Can you go Christmas shopping while your daughter is at volleyball practice? Can your son invite his friends over to play instead of expecting you to take him to the playground? Can you listen to your first-grader read while you wash the car or mend his coat? And remember, it is not always you who must make concessions. Family life is give and take from all.

For some families, outside help is available. In our area, there is a swim program for special children, fulfilling their need for physical exercise and their parents' need for some time away from them. Friends, neighbors or grandparents may be willing to help out. It may mean asking them to babysit or drive a child to soccer practice, or it could just be listening when your child needs to talk. For me, the most marvelous gift was when one of our neighbors showed up at our door during Tom's recuperation from surgery, announcing that she had come to play with him. She spent two hours doing puzzles and playing games with him, giving me a desperately needed break.

After you have done your best to balance everyone's needs, you'll have to admit that the scale still isn't as balanced as you'd like it. You still lead separate lives too often. It is impossible to fully meet everyone's needs and still maintain a healthy family life. So what then?

Compromise and sacrifice! EVERYONE will have to give a little. Is it really necessary for you to sit with your children while they do homework, or can they come to you with their questions? Must you call friends in the evening when your children are expecting calls from school friends? And do you all have to watch television together when you could be reading, writing a letter or catching up on neglected tasks? Some togetherness is necessary, but so is privacy! If everyone gives up a little, unity is gained.

Maintaining balance in your family is an ever-challenging task, changing daily. Those people who share your home are growing, changing individuals. They add excitement and variety—and frustration—to your life. Whether you are a single parent of one child or a married parent of eight, you have a family, a family that cares about you and others.

A healthy family provides the stability necessary to face the challenges of living with a special child. It enriches the life of parents and children and gives them a safe haven in times of distress. Your unique blend of individual needs and family unity is irreplaceable.

Sometimes the task may seem too difficult, the sacrifices too great. But when the scale is once again balanced, you'll know the effort was worth the pain.

Drawing by Ingrid Hodshire, age 15

CHAPTER 6

When Grandpa Talks

A Two-Fold Grief

The diagnosis of a child's special needs affects many people, including grandparents. Grandparents feel a two-fold pain. Of course they grieve for their grandchild. Their dreams have been shattered. But they also grieve for their own child. As parents, they pictured their child having a happy, healthy, wonderful family and saw themselves surrounded by loving, laughing grandchildren. Suddenly they have lost some of these dreams, dreams they had cherished for years. Yes, grandparents grieve. Not the same kind of grief as parents of a special child, but a unique grief that is as important to them as yours is to you.

Changing Times

Any parent knows that grandparents have their own philosophy of child-rearing. Their time-tried methods of discipline or coaxing are willingly offered for our use. We may not always appreciate their help, but we are offered their opinions, anyway.

Things have changed drastically since we were children. Parents now have different philosophies of child-rearing. Working mothers are common today, but may have been rare when you were a child. A mother was totally responsible for care of the home and the well-being of the children. Today, fathers are more involved with the routine tasks and with their children, something grandparents may not understand.

And of course, the biggest change, especially for parents of children with special needs, is the amount of social intervention. There are agencies and organizations who become actively involved in our lives, sometimes overwhelming us. We often do not have the privacy and independence our parents had.

All of this is difficult for grandparents to understand. They remember life as it was when we were children and may have trouble realizing that the rules are different now.

The very definition of a disability has changed. Years ago, only physically handicapped or mentally retarded people were considered disabled. Now we know that there are many types of disabilities, including behavior, learning or medical problems.

Disabled persons were not commonly visible in society years ago, either. They were usually segregated, often in institutions where contact with others was limited. Your child's grandparents probably did not grow up around anyone with a disability and never had a chance to learn how to react in such situations.

Another major change in recent years is the scattering of family members. In the past, grandparents usually lived in the same community as their grandchildren. Even if they lived in different towns, they were usually close enough to visit often. Today, however, our mobile society has left miles between grandparents and their grandchildren. While this may be necessary, it deprives grandparents of regular contact with their grandchildren and allows them few chances to see the children as individuals and adjust to their disabilities.

Different Styles

Grandparents react to special children in different ways. Some grandparents become overprotective. They are overwhelmed with pity for the child. They feel that a child who has to go through so much, shouldn't have to do anything. If you expect anything of your child, you may be labeled unfair or unfeeling. Overprotectiveness is especially common in doomsayers. These are the grandparents who believe the worst before they know anything about the child's condition. "She'll be a vegetable." "He'll never walk." "He'll never do anything in school." They have condemned the child before anyone knows his or her potential.

Other grandparents cannot admit that there is anything seriously wrong with their beautiful grandchild. They think YOU are being overprotective when you refuse to give your nonverbal child something without an effort at communication. They advise you to take a firm line with discipline. That should stop the crying. Or they think you should be more patient, coaxing the child to do something that is still too ambitious for her. These grandparents have not yet faced the reality of your child's condition and may never do so.

Then there are the middle-of-the-road grandparents. They want to help and understand. They try to be compassionate to your situation and take changes in stride. They offer support and advice, but also listen when you explain.

Some grandparents are entrenched in one particular category. Most however, generally fit into one category with occasional slips into others. Their reactions will change with time and with the situation, but their attitudes usually reflect their general outlook.

Grandparents deserve a special kind of consideration that allows both you and them the right to feel pain and joy. When you feel you will scream if Grandma offers one more bit of well-meaning advice, it is time to back away. Don't call or visit for two or three days. Your mate can keep in touch with them if they will worry when they don't hear from you. You don't have to ignore them, just give yourself some time to calm down.

It is important that grandparents have the opportunity to know your child as an individual, giving them a chance to see beyond the disability. Encourage a friendship between them, just as you would any other child. This may require you to give up time alone with your child, but it is better for everyone if you can do so. Grandparents may not care for your child EXACTLY as you do, but unless that poses a real danger to the child, encourage occasional stays.

Any grandparent has advice to offer, advice based on experience and love. The advice may not always be welcome, but it usually is offered in an attempt to help. Whenever possible, listen to their advice. Sometimes they are objective enough to see something we can't. Even if the advice is totally impractical, listen to them. They need to feel a part of your child's life. They suffer many of the same feelings of helplessness that you do, but have even less time with your child. Offering advice, even unwanted advice, may help them cope with the pain of having a grandchild with special needs.

Any parent learns the trick of "tuning out." If necessary, tune them out when you feel you could scream. If they are insistent, repeating the same advice every time you see them, you may need to explain why you haven't done as they suggested. They may not understand, but at least you will have acknowledged their efforts to help.

Like us, grandparents cannot be everything their children need. It's even more difficult to be everything their daughter or son-in-law needs. There will be times when they fail you. Perhaps they don't understand your urgent need for a break or a kind word. Maybe they don't realize that you are under an unusual amount of pressure and just can't handle Christmas dinner. It would be nice if they were always supportive, but that's impossible. Not even your mate can always provide the support you need. Don't be angry with them when they can't help you.

Occasionally, grandparents become over involved in your life. They are so concerned for you and your child that they become intrusive, having too much impact on your life. You can honor their need to be involved, yet still lead your own life. Try to find time just for your family.

If you find grandparents insistent on an impractical idea, you may need to confront them. You don't have to be passive or hostile, but you do need to make your position plain. It may not change the situation, but you will know you have done all you can.

What To Do

Try to realize how grandparents feel. Give them the same understanding that you want. There will be times when they are encouraged by an insignificant accident or devastated by a minor failure. At times they will want to help or will be embarrassed by unusual behavior. There will be times when they could cry from the pain of seeing their grandchild struggle or their child overwhelmed. Allow them these feelings and be as supportive as you would like them to be when you feel the same way.

Don't judge your child's grandparents. Everyone copes with the situation in a different way. It may be frustrating for you when they react differently than you would like, but they have a right to their feelings, just as you do. Give them time.

If they cannot see anything wrong, don't push them. Denial is part of grief. One grandfather could not see why his granddaughter needed speech therapy. It takes time to learn to talk, right? The little girl was ready for preschool and had not yet said a word. The parents felt it was time for action, but it was hard for grandpa. The little girl began therapy, but it was doubly difficult for her parents to cope with the knowledge that she needed help while listening to grandpa insist she was fine.

If your child's grandparents deny the seriousness of your child's condition, don't push them. You can still share your joy in your son's major accomplishments, but don't try to force the grandparents to see what they do not want to see. Don't keep trying to explain that there really is a problem when your nine-month old can't hold up her head. They will have to realize eventually and rushing them will help no one.

If grandparents are overprotective, you may need to downplay problems, even minor ones. One family avoided mentioning their child's persistent low grade fever, even though they knew it could be a sign of a serious infection. They knew that Grandpa and Grandma would be obsessed with worry when it was too early to panic.

The doomsayers will always be difficult to deal with. Try not to let them depress you. You can share your child's accomplishments, but don't discuss potential problems. Wait until something is wrong or you will find yourself reassuring grandparents when you are worried, too.

If your child's grandparents are middle-of-the road, be thankful! There are thousands of parents who envy you. You are able to share more of the highs and lows of parenting a child with special needs. Take care not to overpower them, though. Their emotional position is just as vulnerable as yours.

All grandparents spoil their grandchildren. Rules are different at Grandma's house. There seemed to be an endless supply of cookies at Grandma's house when our boys were younger. Invariably, if we stopped by for a few minutes before dinner, the boys would end up with a cookie in each hand. I worried that they wouldn't eat well when we got home, but I eventually realized that one poor meal wouldn't hurt them. Besides, Grandpa and the boys enjoyed the treat.

Sometimes differences are more serious. One mother worked very hard to curb her son's ploys for attention. If she tried to talk to someone while holding him, he would scream or hit her. Although he was profoundly retarded, she felt this behavior could be stopped. She began laying him on the floor whenever he misbehaved and he soon realized that she would not tolerate his behavior. Grandma, on the other hand, felt that he was entitled to the attention. She felt guilty ignoring him when there were so few things he enjoyed. In just a few hours, Grandma destroyed what the mother had accomplished. The mother found that after every visit to Grandma's she had to start all over again. Grandma was finally informed that if she gave in to the little boy's demands, Mom would immediately take him home, terminating the visit without explanations. After one quick exit, Grandma cooperated. She didn't necessarily agree, but she respected Mom's right to discipline.

Please remember that grandparents want the best for their children and grandchildren. Let them know you appreciate their help—and be gentle when you don't.

Drawing by Meredith Fennell, age 9

CHAPTER 7

Facing The World

It Takes Courage

As we struggle to cope with the pressures and emotions of parenting our special children, our homes become refuges where we can safely hide our fears and grief. Unfortunately, we cannot remain in our homes forever. We must someday venture out into public, facing new trials we may not be prepared for. It takes courage to face the world, to expose ourselves to the potential pain others can inflict, but we must find that courage if we are to resume our lives.

Facing the world means facing friends, neighbors and strangers. It means going out in public, dealing not only with the reactions of others, but also deciding how much of your own pain you will show.

Anything can happen when you "go public." You may encounter stares from people who are not used to seeing a child in a wheelchair. Staring is usually a sign of curiosity, but is not always intended as an insult. Some people automatically stare at anything unusual and forget that there is a real person involved. Others stare out of compassion. They wonder what happened, but do not intentionally insult us.

Families often prefer to use a stroller long past the age a child normally walks, avoiding a wheelchair as long as possible. This makes the family feel less conspicuous, but leaves them open to such comments as "See the baby?" This is especially hurtful when the child being spoken to is younger than the one in the stroller. And of course, children are open in their curiosity. They stare and ask questions, too. They don't mean to be unkind, but it hurts just the same.

Some people are pushy. They want to know everything about your child—even if you aren't ready to tell them. They may not intend to offend you, but do so by denying your right to privacy. They offer unsolicited advice or ask your opinion when you would much rather be inconspicuous.

Others tend to judge us as parents. If our children misbehave or are a little messy, their disapproval shows in their faces or words. And then there are those who put us on a pedestal, proclaiming us to be saintly. "I don't know how you do it," they say.

Perhaps the most difficult people to cope with are those who pity us or our child. They feel sorry for us, but don't know how to handle it. They try to comfort us by telling us that God gave us a special child because He knew we could handle it or remind us that new medical procedures are announced everyday. One family even received a card reading "In your time of sorrow."

Such situations are most common if your child's problem is easily visible. A child with a physical disability is more noticeable than one with a hearing or speech impairment. A child with a behavior disorder attracts more attention than a child with a learning disability. And a child with Down syndrome may draw more stares than another child with mental retardation.

We also encounter problems because of our children's specific needs. Many buildings aren't accessible to children in wheelchairs (or strollers). When one family wanted to redecorate their daughter's bedroom, they went to a department store so she could pick out a new bedspread. They had to enlist the aid of a clerk on the first floor, who led them through a maze of storage shelves to the freight elevator. Ten minutes later, the family reversed the process—after finding that the store had nothing suitable for the little girl's room.

Restaurants also pose difficulties. Many children with special needs cannot eat a regular diet. They must have soft textured food or food without additives. Restaurants often do not have a wide selection of suitable food, leaving parents with the dilemma of how to feed their child or forcing them to pack a special meal before leaving home. And many restaurants put tables so close together that a wheelchair is out of the question. Families must either sit at the drafty table nearest the door, or carry the child in from the car or choose to eat at home.

Dealing With Strangers

Being among strangers poses unique problems. They don't know how to react or what we expect of them. They are as ill-at-ease as we are. Some people want to comfort or sympathize. Some want to know "what happened." Some have a sincere desire to understand and others are just nosey.

There is no firm rule for dealing with strangers. Most parents recommend taking each situation individually. If you are in public and someone seems to be staring, smile at them. If they were being rude, they'll stop. But if they were really interested, they will smile back or speak.

When they ask questions, give them a simple answer. If you aren't prepared to discuss your child's condition, you can then walk away or change the subject. If your questioners are persistent, tell them you'd rather not discuss it.

If you don't mind answering questions, wait for the other people to speak again. If they want more information, they'll ask. Always give short answers, waiting for them to ask for more information. A medical lecture is probably not in order.

Be aware of what is said in front of your child. He or she doesn't need to hear, "poor thing" or "she'll never walk." And don't ignore your child during such conversations. An older child may be capable of answering questions. Let your child become part of the conversation. This is good training for later and also helps dispel the image that a disability is totally disabling.

Do not apologize for your child's disability. If he or she has attracted attention, don't apologize unless damage has been done. If your child broke something or offended someone, an apology should be made. If your child isn't able to apologize, then you should. You should also try to correct your child as you would at home. Sometimes outbursts of hyperactivity or verbal distractions are not avoidable. If there is a drooling problem, quietly wipe your child's face, or remind him or her to do so. Act as if this is perfectly normal (which it is for you) and others will take it in stride, too.

Sometimes strangers can create problems with kindness. There have been several occasions when strangers have offered Tom a dollar or some other gesture of kindness. This has proven to be a two-fold trap for us. We have had to teach Tom not to accept anything unless we approve.

The other problem we have come across is being fair to Tim. There are times when people give Tom extra attention just because of his disability, leaving Tim to wonder if maybe HE isn't the one with the problem. He is left out because he is "normal." That hurts, no matter how old a child is. When this happens, we try to explain to Tim why Tom got the extra attention and to compensate—to make him realize we appreciate his accomplishments. Occasionally both boys are equally involved in an activity, but Tom receives more benefits because of his disability. In such cases we try to distribute the benefits as equally as the work. We also draw him into the conversation if possible. Most people simply want to show their concern and help a child in need. We try to fulfill that goal, but in a different way.

The easiest people to deal with are those who just want to help. These are the people who will wait a few extra seconds to hold a door open for you or pick up something you drop. Sometimes they show they care by saying nothing or by an understanding smile. These people make it easier for us to handle the unpleasant experiences.

If you come across a building that is inaccessible or a restaurant with no appropriate selections, don't be afraid to tell the manager that patronizing the business was difficult for you. Be sure that he or she understands that you would like to shop or dine there, but can't because of the inconvenience. Your comments alone probably won't make a difference, but complaints from several patrons could lead to a change in policy or layout. Until then, you will have to either avoid those places or be prepared for the inconvenience.

Neighbors, Friends and Relatives

Coping with neighbors, friends and relatives can be more difficult. These aren't chance encounters. You must see these people repeatedly and their reactions will have more of an effect on you.

You don't usually choose your neighbors and relatives. You have to cope with them as they are. You will soon learn what their reactions will be. When Tom was born, our neighbors took up a collection to help us fence in our back yard, making it safer for the boys to play and providing us with a little more freedom. To them, Tom was just another child in the neighborhood. They were concerned for his health, but took his condition in stride.

A single father learned to enjoy the concern of his college-age neighbors. He especially appreciated the times the students came over to entertain his son. They even helped out on unique Halloween costumes!

Sometimes neighbors have concerns that have little to do with the welfare of our children. One family had planned to move into a home that could be adapted to their daughter's needs. A few days before the move, they received a phone call from a "friend" in their new neighborhood. They learned that people were upset that such a child would be in their school district and their taxes would have to be used to fund her special education.

You probably have to see relatives several times a year. Your uncle, sister or nephew may be a total bore, making any encounter a dreaded event. They have their own way of looking at your situation and think you should agree. Your sister is vocal in her criticism and adamant in her opinion. Your uncle makes a nuisance of himself and a misery of any family get-together.

Or maybe you have relatives who just can't accept what has happened. They are sorry that you hurt, but they have no intention of sharing your pain. This is hard for you because the pain of having a disabled child is exaggerated by the pain of their indifference.

You don't have to keep silent about your child's disability and its effect on your life just because it makes other people uncomfortable. Mention your disabled child in conversation just as you would any other child. Talk about experiences related to your child's disability as you would other experiences. You don't want to upset others, but casual mention of your situation may help them accept it and will definitely make you feel less overlooked.

If people have other concerns, such as taxes or inconveniences, you can try to explain the situation or the unfairness of their objections. Sometimes, however, nothing will ease their minds and you must try to avoid discussing the particular subject that distresses them.

Friends can be more difficult to deal with. Some relationships don't hold up under the stress. Friends drift away. Some can't face what has happened and must leave. Others don't know what to say or do and the relationship declines. But some manage to cope and the relationship becomes closer, providing support when you most need it. These friends become the refuge you turn to in difficulty.

One of the greatest hazards in any relationship is the saturation point. People may be willing to listen and may care deeply, but there is more to life for them than the trials of parenting a child with special needs. They may be willing to listen, but you must be willing to put some balance in your life, too. You cannot continually complain or overlook the interests and concerns of others.

All relationships change with time. Some grow closer and others won't. It is a sign of your growth and the pattern of life, not a signal of impending trouble. Don't hang on to unfulfilling relationships. Let them flower or wilt naturally, replacing the old with new, more fulfilling relationships.

Facing the world can be difficult. It is always a challenge. And yet friends and strangers are necessary to a happy life. We cannot live as hermits and must encounter both the misery and joy of meeting others. It is up to you to decide how you will cope with these encounters and how much they affect you. YOU are in control and how you exercise that control will help determine how happy you will be.

CHAPTER 8

Working With Professionals

Co-Workers

If your child has special needs, you are going to have to work with specialists from several fields. For many parents, coping with professionals can be overwhelming. While attempting to find answers to their child's problem and contend with an unfamiliar situation, they often fall into the "doctor is God" syndrome. This isn't good for the child, the parent or the professional. It's easy to do, but must be avoided.

At a time when you are feeling especially helpless, you are exposed to people with years of training. They must know the answers, you think. After all, they have studied and worked with similar cases before. Therefore, they are smarter than you and you have to do whatever they say. Right? WRONG!

Those you work with, including doctors, are not gods. They are not all-powerful or all-knowing. They are human beings, just like you. Their knowledge and expertise deserve your respect, not your worship.

A professional is not your boss, either. You are co-workers, neither more important than the other. You may never become friends, but neither should you be adversaries.

Different Perspectives

In working with professionals, keep in mind that they are ordinary people. They have families, worries and interests just like everyone else. Their world does not exist solely in the clinic or office, even though it may seem they expect yours to at times.

Everybody has a different outlook on the world depending on personal experiences. This includes professionals. These experiences color every aspect of our lives, affecting how we see the world and our reaction to it.

For instance, one little girl is afraid of clowns. Clowns generally delight children with their antics, but this child is terrified of them. When a clown visits the pediatrics unit most of the young patients are thrilled with the balloon animals and tricks, but one little girl will huddle at the edge of bed, waiting anxiously for the visit to end. The clown has done nothing to frighten her, but she wants him to leave. Why? Perhaps something has happened to make her afraid of clowns. Or maybe nothing in the past has prepared her for such an unusual stranger. She is like other children, except that past experiences have made her fear clowns.

Some children also fear Santa Claus which can be especially frustrating and embarrassing for parents. If your child, for some unknown reason, were frightened by these normally enticing characters, you would try to be understanding.

We try to be understanding of our children, yet can fail to extend the same courtesy to others. A short tempered therapist may have just come from a session with an uncooperative child. An unresponsive doctor may have gotten very little sleep because of emergency calls. It's unfair to expect professionals to be always in tune with your thoughts and needs. If they were, their patients wouldn't be individuals to them, and they wouldn't care so much about them.

Misunderstandings can sometimes be trivial. For example, it has always struck me as particularly silly when doctors walk into an examining room and ask, "How are you?" Obviously, I wouldn't be there if I were fine. What do they expect me to say? For the doctor, it's simply a way of saying, "I'm here and I'm ready to examine you." Personally, I think a simple "good afternoon" would do, but then I'm not faced with several similar situations in the same day. Our experiences differ, and so do our interpretations of routine greetings.

Misunderstandings can also be quite serious, though. Our son was hospitalized for weeks following his birth and for much of that time death was a very real possibility. When we called the doctor to ask how our baby was, he told us, "He's holding his own." I was crushed. My newborn infant was in a hospital miles away and was struggling for each breath. To me, "holding his own" meant that he was not improving; he was not moving toward life. But to the doctor, "holding his own" meant that Tom was holding on; that my little boy was battling death and putting up a fair fight. He was not giving in to a tough opponent. "Holding his own" was good news to the doctor, devastating news to me—until I realized what he meant.

If a simple greeting or phrase can be misunderstood, think how much easier it is to confuse complex conversations. When you give information to the doctor, you are talking about your experiences with your child from YOUR viewpoint. When the doctor asks questions, is it an expression of doubt or an effort to get more information? In the same way, your questions can be misinterpreted. Are you questioning the physicians authority and knowledge?

What To Do

It is possible and advantageous to have honest communication between professionals and parents, but only in an atmosphere of mutual respect for each other's perspective.

Professionals as well as parents want to develop good working relationships for the benefit of the child. They care about your child's welfare and want to work with you. There are some things that you, as a parent, can do to help set the tone of any professional relationship and foster cooperation.

First, learn all you can about your child's problem. Read any information available and talk to other parents. If a medical social worker is available, ask for additional sources of information.

It's a good idea to make a list of questions and concerns you want to talk over with the professional. If possible, discuss it with your mate to be sure you have listed everything and know exactly what information you want. An increasing number of professionals are taking time to chat with parents, giving them a chance to share concerns. If you feel you are being rushed or that someone is not giving you the time you need, it's okay to be assertive. You don't have to get nasty. Just say you have more questions.

Some parents have no problems when communicating with professionals—unless the professional is a doctor. Remember, doctors are no different than the others you work with. They may have more education, an impressive title or some renown in their field, but they are still people.

I have the most difficulty communicating with the professionals at my son's school. We see the doctor only a few times each year, but are in contact with the school regularly. I have trouble voicing my opinions when I know they are in conflict with those of the therapist, teacher or other professional. I want to maintain my "nice mom" image yet still be heard—something that can be almost impossible at times. And, like all parents, I sometimes face the frustration of failing to do what I know I should simply because I lack confidence.

If you are working with professionals who tend to use highly technical language, tell them that you don't understand and ask for explanations. You can also rephrase the statement in your own words and then ask if you have understood correctly. As a parent, you have an obligation to learn as much as possible about your child's condition, but you cannot be expected to know as much as the doctor, therapist or other specialist. These people are sources of information as well as treatment. You have a need and a right to fully understand what they are saying. Asking questions increases your knowledge and that, in return, actually helps the professionals. Keep asking until you understand.

If you are working with an individual who says very little and appears ready to leave the appointment without telling you much of anything, it's your responsibility to ask questions. "Is there a reason why my child sleeps so much?" "Is my daughter's vision deteriorating?" Make your questions as specific to your child's condition as possible. Again, you are the caregiver of this child and you have every right to be assertive in seeking a consultation following an examination or treatment.

When a test or course of treatment is prescribed, ask questions. "What will the test show?" "Will my son be in any pain?" "Is there any medication involved?" Even, "How much will it cost?" Find out all you can before giving permission for something you are not sure about. If the recommended treatment or test is vital to your child's health, of course you will agree. On the other hand, there may be times when you feel it is best not to approve something. Your child's condition may not have changed enough to warrant repeating an uncomfortable test. Maybe a treatment will cause more pain than the results make worthwhile. Or, maybe your child has just had enough of being fussed with for a while. If you feel a procedure is not in the best interest of your son or daughter, tell the professional involved. Just be sure to explain your reasons for withholding permission. Remember, professionals could feel threatened if you question their recommendations. They may be able to explain why it is important that the treatment or test be done immediately or they may agree that it can wait. They may not agree with you at all, but if your child's immediate health or long term progress is not at stake, you have the right to say "no."

If your child sees several professionals, you may find that their expectations for what you can do are unrealistic. Usually, professionals recommend what is ideal within their speciality. But, often they are not aware of the recommendations of other professionals, leaving you feeling as though they expect the impossible. The orthopedist says, "Exercise her legs three times a day." The speech pathologist recommends daily directed conversations about household objects, the nutritionist recommends six small meals a day and the teacher sends home three pages of homework and a list of spelling words. No one demand is too great, but put them all together and you spend most of your time with your child doing what other people expect. There is no time left to simply enjoy being together. If this happens, tell the professionals involved. That's the only way they can know what is happening. If possible, they may adjust their demands according to your schedule. Your child's greatest need is to be loved. You must always be sure there is enough time for that.

There is rarely, if ever, reason to be accusing or belligerent with a professional. Usually, differences of opinion can be handled by firmly and calmly voicing your feelings to the professional involved. Say, "I have other questions and I would appreciate it if you would stay and answer them." Or, "I don't think you are taking this new symptom seriously enough." You are not attacking someone when you say clearly what you are feeling.

On rare occasions, it is impossible to work with certain people. They may not give you the respect you deserve or you may have lost respect for them. A social worker, if available, may help in this case. Also, try to understand how the professional views the situation. Maybe there is something you can do or say to improve the relationship. If you feel there is nothing you can do, it may be necessary to change doctors or other professionals. Usually, there are other doctors or therapists qualified to handle your child's care. If you find you simply cannot work with one, then quietly find another. If you change treatment centers, you should write to the administrator, explaining why you left. Perhaps other parents are having the same problem.

If, for any reason, you change professionals, tell your new therapist or doctor about your child's past evaluations. This can help avoid repeating unnecessary tests and examinations, sparing your child discomfort and you expense.

Because professionals are not gods, they cannot know everything. Don't expect them to. A competent professional, especially a doctor, will be continually reading and learning about new developments within a specialty. But no one can be expected to know everything. A doctor who prescribes a treatment for your child that doesn't work has not willingly erred, but has simply chosen the treatment that seemed to have the greatest chance of success. It might have been wrong, but it wasn't intentional.

If you want doctors and others to be understanding of your weaknesses, then you must be understanding of theirs. If something doesn't turn out the way you think it should, tell the professional involved, but do it nicely. They are probably disappointed too.

While minor errors in judgment are understandable, there is never an excuse for incompetence. A professional should have adequate knowledge, skills and dedication to give your child the treatment he or she deserves. If your professional seems incompetent, talk to the social worker, administrator or regulating agency in your area.

The key to a good working relationship with anyone is respect, and the relationships between you and the professionals working with your child are not exceptions.

They are not gods and do not know everything. They know about your child's condition but not about your child. YOU are the expert on your child. And without complete cooperation from everyone, your child cannot receive the best care possible. Work with professionals toward your common goal--your child's well-being.

Drawing by Megan Donovan, age 3

CHAPTER 9

More Than A Parent

There's More To Life

When you have a child with special needs it's easy to be overwhelmed. It's not just the work; it's the worry and pressure. Your life seems to be guided by circumstances, not your will. Being a parent becomes the most important thing in your life.

Being a parent IS important, but shouldn't be the only important thing in anyone's life. You must maintain your individuality, your awareness of yourself. Not only is this necessary to your happiness, it is necessary to being a good parent.

Devoting yourself exclusively to your child really doesn't help anyone. For you, it means suppressing your needs, wants and dreams. For your special child, it means you can no longer see the situation realistically, impairing your judgment and becoming overprotective. For others in your family, it means neglect and hurt. You don't have the energy or interest you used to have. Being consumed by your special child isn't fair to anyone. You must be an individual, nurturing your unique talents, interests and feelings. You must be more than a parent.

Be Good To Yourself

Being a parent is a time-consuming job and it's easy to become driven by necessary tasks, overlooking other pleasant, and rewarding aspects of your life. When this happens, take time for yourself. You may have to ask for help or admit that you are feeling frustrated, but it's worth it. Many parents have suffered anxiety attacks from the stress, leaving them shaky, tearful or physically ill. Learn constructive ways to cope with the stress for your own sake.

Get to know yourself again. Think about yourself, your dreams and your goals. Then plan what you can do to make your life more fulfilling. Each day, try to take one small step toward that goal.

If you feel restless when you are alone, try to remember what you enjoyed before your child was born. Did you read? Did you restore cars? Or did you study the works of great artists? You might enjoy these pursuits now if you made the time.

Treat yourself occasionally. Take yourself to lunch instead of grabbing a sandwich. Buy that book you want to read, or check it out at the library. Then make sure you read it. Indulge yourself once in a while; you're worth it!

Take pride in your appearance. It's easy to let your appearance go in your attempt to cope with your special child, but your appearance is just as important as your childs. Don't settle for rundown, unkempt clothes. Keep your clothing neat and in good repair. Keep your hair cut, your face shaved and your shoes polished. Moms, don't neglect make-up. If you wore it before, wear it now! It's important to feel good about yourself.

You need to take care of your body, too. Eat properly, making a point of cooking nutritious meals instead of grabbing a bag of potato chips. Make a point of getting adequate sleep every night and exercising regularly. If you're not feeling well, go to the doctor. Even if money is tight, you should seek medical help. If you are ill you won't be as good a parent and a little care now could prevent more serious illness later.

It is also important to spend time with other adults. The stimulation of their conversation can help you keep a sense of reality and provide an escape from your worries and responsibilities.

Enjoy Yourself

Parenting a special child doesn't have to be all worry and work. Allow yourself to enjoy your child. One family made construction paper chains while the youngster was in a standing brace, turning tedious minutes into constructive fun. When one little boy resisted coming inside as told, his father joined him in the pile of autumn leaves.

Enjoy just being with your child once in a while. Give yourself permission to laugh, even when a rule is broken. Or rock your child to sleep, even though he or she is getting a little old for that. The worries and responsibilities will still be there, but for a few minutes, you will have experienced peace and companionship with your child.

It's easier to enjoy your child if you take a break from your duties occasionally. If you don't, you'll become more of a nurse than a parent, losing the ability to value his or her uniqueness. If you can hire a babysitter or ask a friend to take over for a short time, do it! If you can't, then take a break at home. Pursue a hobby or develop a talent during naps or while your child is occupied with a toy.

Forgive Yourself

Forgive yourself when you have feelings you didn't expect. All parents resent their children at times or tire of coping with their problems. Admit it when you do, then forgive yourself. Feeling guilty takes time and energy but accomplishes nothing.

Even the most competent parent goofs occasionally. More than one parent has forgotten a pill or skipped an exercise. Even the most loving parent has lost his temper. Chances are, none of these will seriously or permanently harm your child. You can regret your mistake and try to avoid repeating it, but you must allow

yourself to be human. Forgive yourself as you would
someone else. You can't laugh unless you know how to
cry or snarl.

Outside Interests

For some parents, especially mothers, whether to
work outside the home is a difficult question. In our
society, it is still expected that the mother will give the
majority of care to children. It is hard to deal with the
normal problems of being a working mom plus the extra
worries of parenting a special child. But working gives us
a much-needed feeling of usefulness. It helps us feel
more competent and provides added income.

It can be difficult, though, to find the right job. A
single mother tried several times to find a job, but just
when she found something that would allow her to be
home after school, her little girl got sick. The mother
needed and wanted to work, but just couldn't find a
position that allowed her to be a good mother and
employee.

Some parents find an outlet in volunteer work.
This work may be for an agency that serves children with
disabilities, but it could also be a church, civic organiza-
tion or school. It helps maintain your sense of worth if
you can contribute something.

Volunteering can become a trap, though. It's too
easy to take on projects, leaving little or no time for
relaxation. Many parents find this to be a big problem
because the feeling of being needed offsets the feelings of
helplessness they have with their child. Don't be afraid
to say "no" before you are overwhelmed.

Remember, the best thing you can do for your
family is to take care of yourself. When you are happy,
healthy and fulfilled, you will be the best parent possible.
To be a good parent, you must be more than a parent!